INTRODUCTION

On the humid, sticky Miami morning of November 23, 2000, I raced anxiously through my Grandmother Georgia Bell's kitchen, gathering ingredients for my special dish. It was Thanksgiving Day, and I'd promised my mom, Sandra, I would make the best sweet potato pie she'd ever tasted, if she would just give me a chance. The pressure was on, and I was determined to solidify my spot as an annual contributor to my family's holiday dinners. As I scrambled, my mom watched, patiently offering advice on the small things along the way.

Even as we celebrated touchdowns on the living room television, laughed as loud as we could in the dining room, and dived into the turkey my dad made, I had butterflies in the pit of my stomach the entire day. This was, after all, a make or break moment for me: I could end this day as the crowned king of sweet potato pies, with bragging rights to last a lifetime, or I could be forever banned from the kitchen during holidays for the rest of my life. Granted, in retrospect, my thought process was a little dramatic, but, in my thirteen-year-old mind, this was my reality. My hands trembled as I brought the first piece up to my mouth….and it was AMAZING! Then I thought, it was amazing to me, but what was everyone else thinking? As I continued to devour my slice, I slyly began to survey the room. There is a science to testing your success as a kid chef. My family has always been supportive, so I couldn't gauge their satisfaction based on just compliments or clean plates. I patiently awaited that one action confirming my holiday dessert spot was secure, then it happened. I knew for sure I was successful the moment my dad got a second slice. That day is still one of my favorite memories. Everyone was so happy and

pleasantly surprised, and it was one of the first times I felt truly accomplished. At that moment, I learned that cooking was my passion.

As the years passed, I continued to fall more and more in love with baking and used those bragging rights I had earned every chance I got. When I became a high school student, I decided it was time to step it up a notch. My dad had been a firehouse chef for the City of Miami my entire life, and I felt ready to soak up all his knowledge. By my sophomore year, I had graduated to the meats, and cooking quickly became bonding time with my dad. Whether it was in the kitchen or outside on the grill, I was with him, taking note of every detail he was willing to offer. Not only was I learning recipes, but I was also learning life lessons from him. My dad had mastered the balance between superhero and loving family man. He fascinated me, so much so that I decided to follow in his footsteps by becoming a firefighter. I wasn't sure if I'd come even remotely close to being the man he was, but I knew it'd be my biggest regret if I didn't try.

In 2007, I became a proud member of the City of Orlando Fire Department in Orlando, FL. All twenty-one of the guys at Fire House No. 1 welcomed me with open arms, and our friendships became family ties in no time. Turns out, they even trusted me to cook, and they loved it! Dinner at the fire house echoed dinner with my dad: it was a time to bond, laugh, and relax. Those firehouse experiences are the inspiration behind this book: I want to help you create those same memories. Trust me; there's nothing better than good food and loud laughter. From the family chef to the rookie, don't worry, Chef Manny is in your house today, and I've got something for everybody. Let's put some flames on 'em!

ACKNOWLEDGEMENTS

To My Wife, Vanessa, thank you for your support and inspiration

Manny with USAR

©2020 Chef Manny FD

All rights reserved. This book or parts thereof may not be reproduced in any form, stored in any retrieval system, or transmitted in any form by any means—electronic, mechanical, photocopy, recording, or otherwise—without prior written permission of the publisher, except as provided by United States of America copyright law. For permission requests, write to the publisher, at "Attention: Permissions Coordinator," at the address below.

ISBN: 978-1-7363077-1-7

Book design and food photography: ©Alexi Shields | Chomp Chomp Studios LLC

To My Family and Friends Thank You for pushing me and believing in me before there was even " Chef Manny FD".

Manny with Friends

To my fellow firefighters from around the world, thank you for serving and making this world a safe place. To the Orlando Fire Department thank you for hiring me at 19 years old and helping mold the man I am today.

TABLE OF CONTENTS

1st Alarm – Appetizers / Sides
Baked Goat Cheese w/ Crostini
Macaroni and Cheese
Coconut Rice
Bacon-Wrapped Asparagus
Cornbread
Garlic Mash Potatoes
Fiesta Chorizo Sliders

2nd Alarm- Entrees
This Ain't your Mama's Meatloaf
Chimichurri Steak
Firehouse Burger w/ Bacon Jam
Chicken Teriyaki
Red Wine Braised Short Ribs
Bombero Sandwich (Cuban Sandwich)
Firehouse Chili
Blackened Salmon

3rd Alarm- Desserts/ Breakfast
Bread Pudding w Marshmallow Sauce
Cheesecake
Pound Cake with Pineapple Cherry Flambé
Stuffed French Toast with strawberry sauce
Key Lime Pancakes

1st Alarm Starters & Sides

Picture this: you're in the middle of your regular day to day work routine, and the phone rings. You answer, and the voice on the other end says they're calling from the Food Network and would like to invite you to participate in a major show. Weirdest thing ever, right? So I did what anyone else would do: I hung up, grumbled about who still does prank calls in the new millennium, and hopped right back into my routine. Then the phone rang again, and the caller assured me she was serious; apparently, my firehouse family submitted me to compete in the hit show Cutthroat Kitchen. A few weeks later, the entire world was watching me make chili cheese fries with a crowbar. Between you and I, I was thoroughly confused about how I'd landed on the show for the entire duration of the competition. There was no time to figure it out though, I had to focus all my energy on winning. When I was announced as the winner, I was stunned, in fact, I'm still stunned. Reality didn't even begin to sink in until well after the show ended. I'd made my dad so proud; I'd made my firehouse family proud, and I'm ready to share that feeling with you. We'll begin with a few starters and sides, don't back down from the first alarm. Remember, at least you can use more than a crowbar.

INGREDIENTS

1 10-ounce log goat cheese, at room temperature
4 ounces cream cheese, at room temperature
1/4 cup grated parmesan cheese
1/4 cup extra-virgin olive oil
Freshly ground pepper
8 small cocktail tomatoes (about 10 ounces), quartered
2 tbsp. chopped fresh chives
2 tsp. white balsamic vinegar
1 clove garlic, finely chopped
Kosher salt
Toasted baguette slices, for serving

DIRECTIONS

Preheat the oven to 400° F. Combine the goat cheese, cream cheese, parmesan, garlic, and 2 tablespoons olive oil in a food processor and season with pepper; puree until smooth. Brush a 1-quart baking dish with olive oil, then spread the cheese mixture in the dish, mounding it slightly higher around the edge than in the middle. Bake until golden and heated through, about 15 minutes. Meanwhile, combine the tomatoes, chives, vinegar, garlic, the remaining 2 tablespoons of olive oil, and 1/2 teaspoon salt in a medium bowl. Spoon the tomato mixture on top of the dip. Serve with baguette slices.

SERVES: 4-6 FIREFIGHTERS

BAKED GOAT CHEESE
with Crostini

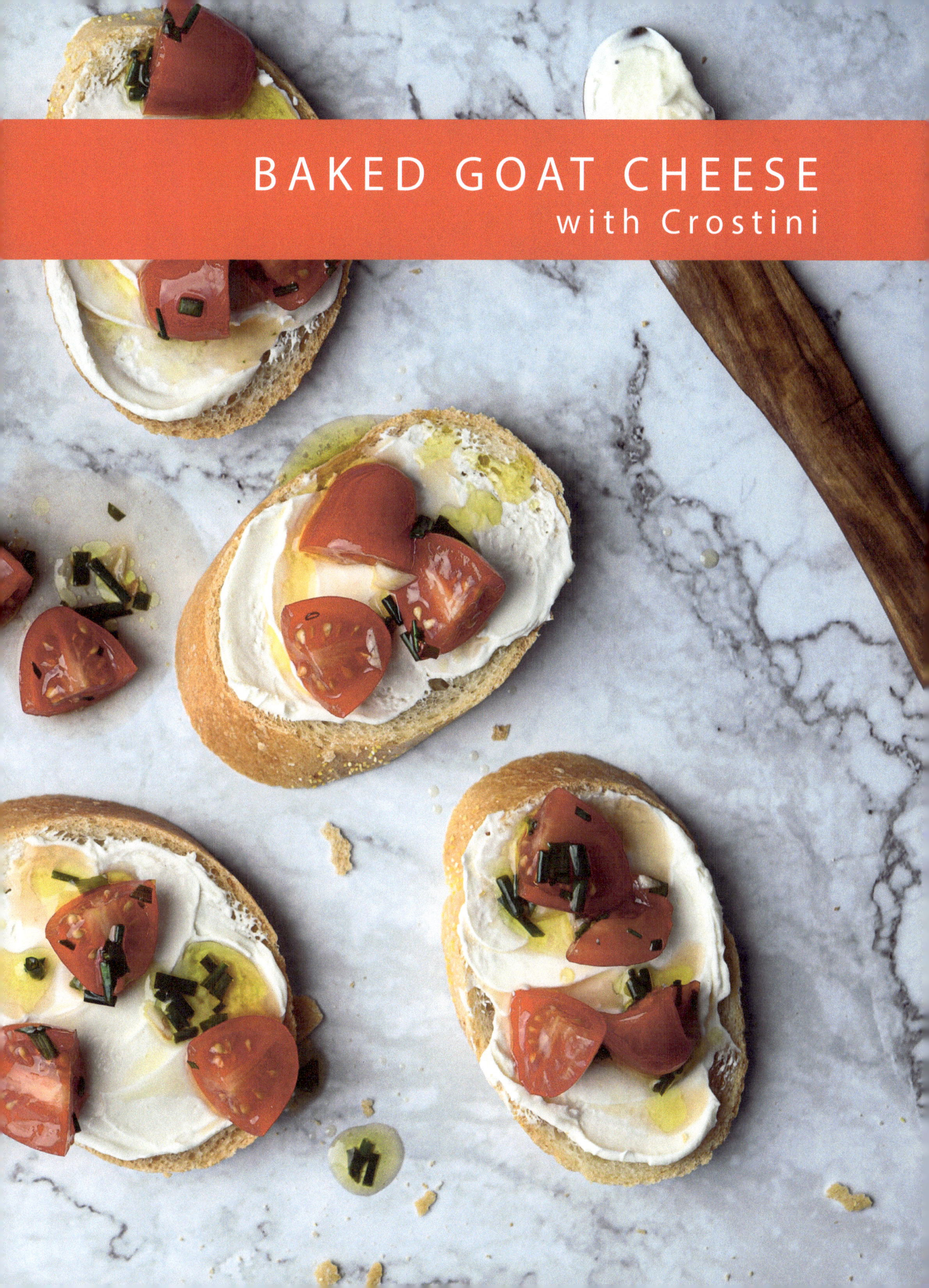

INGREDIENTS

1 lb. dried penne pasta
1/2 cup unsalted butter
1/2 cup all-purpose flour
1 1/2 cups heavy cream
2 1/2 cups whole milk
4 cups grated medium sharp cheddar cheese
4 cups grated colby jack cheese
½ cup of goat cheese
1 cup cream cheese
½ cup of sour cream
½ tbsp. salt
½ tbsp. black pepper
½ tbsp. granulated garlic
½ tbsp. paprika

DIRECTIONS

Preheat oven to 350°F and add nonstick spray onto a 9x13 baking pan.

Bring a large pot of salted water to a boil. When boiling, add dried pasta and cook 1 minute less than the package directs for al dente.

Melt butter in a large saucepan over medium heat. Sprinkle in flour and whisk to combine. Cook for approximately 1 minute, whisking often.
Slowly pour in heavy cream while whisking constantly, until smooth.
Slowly pour in the milk while whisking constantly, until combined and smooth.
Continue to heat over medium heat, whisking very often until thickened.

Drop to low heat add 2 cups of each (cheddar cheese and colby jack cheese), stir until melted.

MACARONI AND CHEESE

Add cream cheese, goat cheese, and sour cream to the sauce. Add salt pepper and garlic powder to sauce. In a large mixing bowl,
combine drained pasta with cheese sauce, stirring to combine fully.
Pour pasta mixture into the prepared baking dish. Top with the rest of the cheeses (cheddar and colby jack)
Sprinkle paprika on top of the mac and cheese. Bake for 15-20 minutes, until cheesy is bubbly and lightly golden brown.

SERVES: 4 FIREFIGHTERS

INGREDIENTS

2 cups of coconut milk
1 cup of Jasmine rice
1/2 cup of coconut shreds
1 tbsp. of butter

DIRECTIONS

Place coconut milk in a saucepan on high heat with coconut shred and butter. Allow milk to heat until almost boiling (WATCH OUT FOR BOILOVER WITH MILK). Add in rice stir, bring down to low heat, and cover and cook for 30 minutes until done.

SERVES: 5 FIREFIGHTERS

COCONUT RICE

INGREDIENTS

Asparagus
1-pound asparagus ends trimmed
2 tbsp. olive oil
Kosher salt to taste
8 slices bacon cut in half
Fresh ground black pepper
1 lemon cut in half
1 tbsp. of minced garlic

DIRECTIONS

FOR THE BALSAMIC GLAZE
½-cup light brown sugar
2 cups balsamic vinegar

Bacon-Wrapped Asparagus
Preheat oven to 400°F.
Place asparagus on a baking sheet add oil, salt, pepper, garlic. Mix well.
Wrap a slice of bacon around each asparagus spear in a spiral.
Line up on a baking sheet and squeeze the fresh lime juice over the asparagus.
Place in oven for 10 minutes and flip to cook for another 10 minutes or until desired crispiness

FOR THE BALSAMIC GLAZE
Heat balsamic vinegar and brown sugar in a small pot or saucepan over medium heat.
Bring to a gentle boil, and then reduce heat to medium-low heat and let simmer, stirring occasionally until the vinegar thickens and is reduced to about 1 cup (about 10 minutes). It should be thick enough to coat the back of a spoon.
Remove from heat and allow to cool (Glaze will thicken)
Garnish asparagus with glaze

SERVES: 4 FIREFIGHTERS

BACON WRAPPED ASPARAGUS

INGREDIENTS

1 1/2 cups cornmeal
1 cup all-purpose flour
1/3 cup sugar
4 tsp. baking powder
1 tsp. kosher salt
2 cups buttermilk
1 cup of creamed corn
1 large egg
6 tbsp. unsalted butter, melted and divided

DIRECTIONS

Preheat oven to 425° F. Place an oven-proof 10-inch cast-iron skillet in the oven.
In a large bowl, combine cornmeal, flour, sugar, baking powder, and salt.
In a large glass measuring cup or another bowl, whisk together buttermilk, creamed corn, and 3 tablespoons of butter. Pour mixture over dry ingredients and stir using a rubber spatula just until moist.
Remove skillet from the oven and add remaining 3 tablespoons until heated through, about 1-2 minutes.
Working carefully, immediately scoop the batter into the hot skillet. Place into oven and bake for 25-30 minutes, or until a tester inserted in the center comes out.

SERVES: 4 FIREFIGHTERS

CORNBREAD

INGREDIENTS

2 ½ lb. potatoes (red), peeled
Sea salt and black pepper
2 tbsp. butter
1 bunch of green onions (about 6-8), trimmed and chopped
2 tbsp. minced garlic
¾ cup whipping cream
¾ cup whole milk
1 tbsp. dried Rosemary
1 tbsp. of dried thyme
4 quarts of water

DIRECTIONS

Cut the potatoes into similar-size chunks
Boil in water for about 15 minutes until tender. Drain well.

In a separate sauce pan, add milk, cream, garlic, butter, sour cream, cream cheese, parmesan cheese, rosemary and thyme on simmer.
Mash the potatoes while still hot into a mixing bowl, using a potato ricer or just smash.
Stir in simmering milk mixture little by little until smooth mash potatoes.

SERVES: 4-6 FIREFIGHTERS

GARLIC MASH POTATOES

INGREDIENTS

1 pound ground beef
4 ounces chorizo sausage, casing removed
2 tsp. onion powder
1 tsp. ground cumin, plus 1 tsp. for the sauce
Salt and pepper
1 cup grated aged Cheddar
1 cup queso Blanco
1/2 cup mayonnaise
1/4 cup ketchup
1 lime, zested and juiced
6 slider buns, split

DIRECTIONS

In a medium bowl, mix the ground beef, chorizo, onion powder, cumin, and 2 teaspoons each salt and pepper. Form the mixture into palm-sized balls.

Heat a griddle or large skillet over medium-high heat. Place the balls on the griddle and smash with a spatula or the back of a spoon. Cook, flipping once until cooked through. Divide the Cheddar and queso blanco among the burgers and let melt. Remove the burgers to a plate.

Meanwhile, combine the mayonnaise, ketchup and lime zest, and juice in a bowl; mix to blend. Add cumin, salt and pepper to taste.

Toast the slider buns on the griddle. Serve the burgers on the buns, topped with some rosada sauce.

SERVES: 3 FIREFIGHTERS

FIESTA CHORIZO SLIDERS

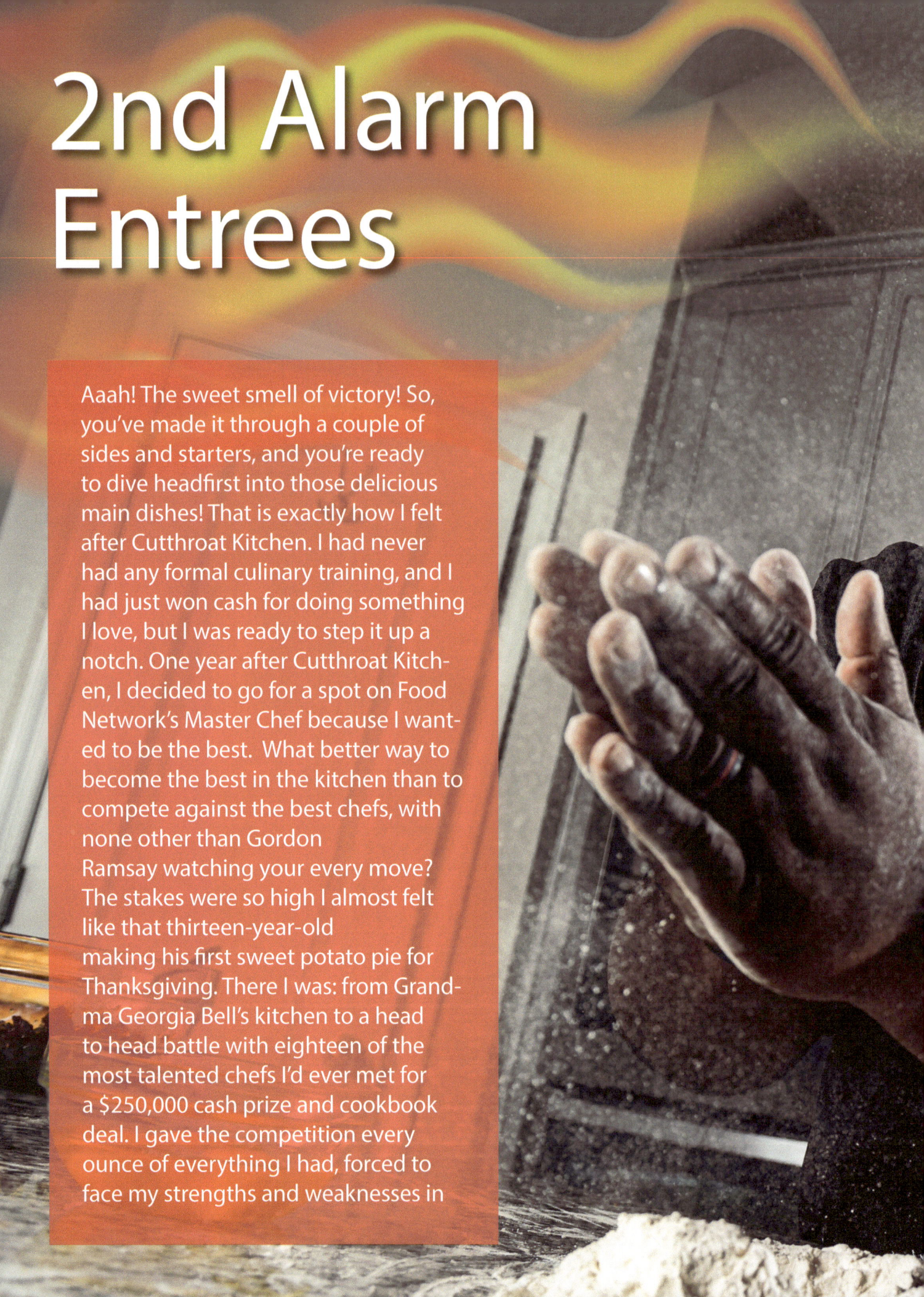

2nd Alarm Entrees

Aaah! The sweet smell of victory! So, you've made it through a couple of sides and starters, and you're ready to dive headfirst into those delicious main dishes! That is exactly how I felt after Cutthroat Kitchen. I had never had any formal culinary training, and I had just won cash for doing something I love, but I was ready to step it up a notch. One year after Cutthroat Kitchen, I decided to go for a spot on Food Network's Master Chef because I wanted to be the best. What better way to become the best in the kitchen than to compete against the best chefs, with none other than Gordon Ramsay watching your every move? The stakes were so high I almost felt like that thirteen-year-old making his first sweet potato pie for Thanksgiving. There I was: from Grandma Georgia Bell's kitchen to a head to head battle with eighteen of the most talented chefs I'd ever met for a $250,000 cash prize and cookbook deal. I gave the competition every ounce of everything I had, forced to face my strengths and weaknesses in

the process. But that's what cooking is all about, it's about taking risks to find what works for you.
Welcome to the process! Not only are you going to walk away with the
secret to my chimichurri steak recipe I used to nail the Master Chef audition, but I'm also going to share a few of my methods to spice up
popular every day dishes like meatloaf and hamburgers.
You know what time it is:
time to put some flames on 'em!

photo by Greg Gayne

THIS AIN'T YOUR MAMA'S MEATLOAF

INGREDIENTS

2 tbsp. of olive oil
1 cup puréed yellow onions (1 whole onions)
1 cup puréed red pepper (2 peppers)
1 cup puréed green pepper (2 peppers)
1 tsp. chopped fresh thyme leaves
2 tsp. kosher salt
1 tsp. freshly ground black pepper
3 tbsp. Worcestershire sauce
1/3 cup chicken stock
1 tbsp. tomato paste
2 1/2 pounds ground chuck (80 percent lean)
1 cup frosted Corn flakes
3 extra-large eggs, beaten
Ketchup
1 cup of Bacon Jam

DIRECTIONS

Preheat the oven to 325° F.
Heat the olive oil in a medium sauté pan.
Add the onions, red and green peppers thyme, salt, and pepper and cook over medium-low heat, stirring occasionally, for 8 to 10 minutes, until the onions are translucent but not brown.
Off the heat, add the Worcestershire sauce, chicken stock, and tomato paste. Allow to cool slightly.
In a large bowl, combine the ground chuck, onion mixture, corn flakes, eggs, and mix.
Shape the mixture into a rectangular loaf on a sheet pan covered with parchment paper.
Spread the ketchup evenly on top.
Bake for 1 to 1 1/4 hours, until the internal temperature is 160° F and the meat-loaf is cooked through.
Once completed, spoon on bacon jam.

SERVES: 6 FIREFIGHTERS

CHIMICHURRI STEAK

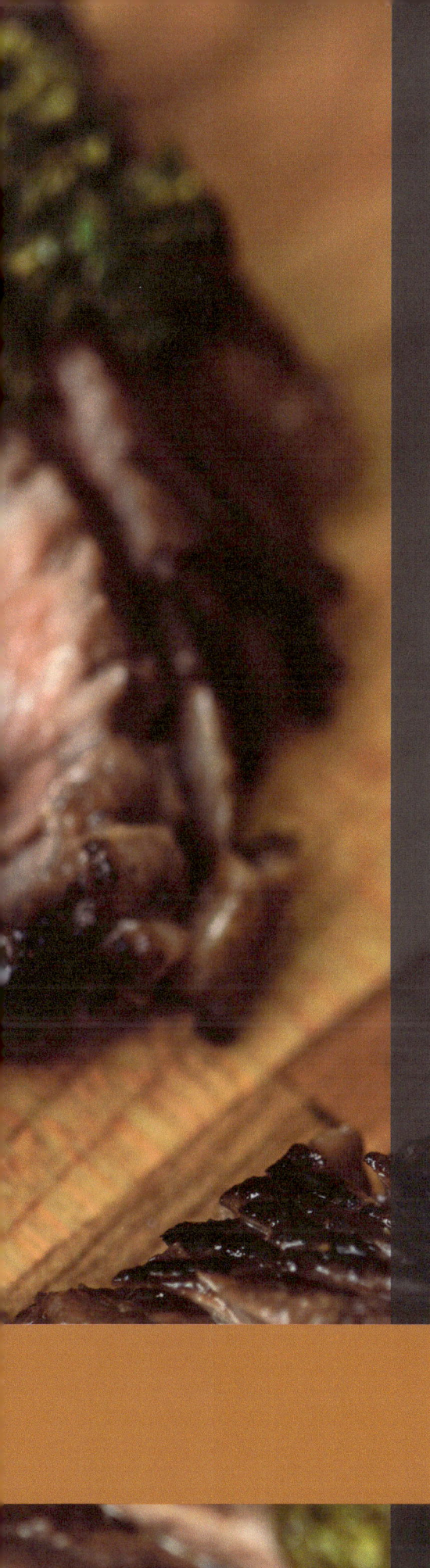

INGREDIENTS

2 pounds skirt steak, trimmed of excess fat
2 limes, plus 1 extra lime for serving
1 orange
1 lemon
2/3 cup olive oil, divided
4 medium cloves garlic, minced
1 teaspoon ground cumin
Kosher salt and freshly ground black pepper
2 tbsp. Worchestire sauce
Chimichurri Sauce
1 cup dried parsley
½ cup fresh cilantro chopped
1/3 cup extra virgin olive oil
2 tbsp. red wine vinegar
1/2 tsp. sea salt
1/8 tsp. freshly ground black pepper
1/4 tsp. red pepper flakes
Juice of ½ lime

DIRECTIONS

Combine ingredients place on skirt steak in a bowl. Marinate no longer than 24 hours. When ready to grill, pat dry of marinade to prevent steaming. Grill on high heat 3-4 minutes on each side until
medium rare-medium on grill until golden brown and perfectly charred then allow to rest before slicing on a cutting board.

Chimichurri Sauce
Combine ingredients and top skirt steak after slicing.

SERVES: 6 FIREFIGHTERS

FIREHOUSE BURGER w/ Bacon Jam

INGREDIENTS

1 pound bacon
1/2 white onion, chopped
1/3 cup dark brown sugar
1/2 cup apple cider vinegar
1 bunch roughly chopped fresh thyme leaves
Burger:
1 pound ground beef
2 tbsp. salt
2 tbsp. pepper
Grapeseed oil, for cooking the burger
4 slices American cheese
4 slices cheddar cheese
4 hamburger buns, toasted
1/2 cup mayonnaise
1/2 cup arugula

DIRECTIONS

BACON JAM

Cook the bacon in a large nonstick skillet over medium-high heat, stirring occasionally, until browned and crisp, and the fat has rendered out. Allow to cool, then chop the bacon.

In the same pan with the bacon drippings, add the onions and cook, stirring occasionally until slightly softened. Add the brown sugar, vinegar, and thyme; bring to a simmer. Reduce the heat to low and cook until the liquid is absorbed and the mixture has thickened to a jam-like consistency, about 20 minutes. Stir in the bacon; remove from the heat.

BURGER

Divide the beef into 4 equal portions and form into burger patties. Sprinkle both sides of each patty with salt and pepper.

Heat the oil in a pan or griddle over high heat. Cook the patties until golden brown and slightly charred on the first side, about 3 minutes. Flip over the patties and cook until golden brown and slightly charred on the second side or to the desired degree of doneness, about 4 minutes for medium-rare. Add 1 slice of American cheese and 1 slice of cheddar to the top of each patty during the last

minute of cooking, then top the pan with a basting cover or tent the patties with aluminum foil to melt the cheese.

Coat the bottom of the buns with mayo. Put the patties on the mayo-coated buns and top with the arugula and bacon jam. Sandwich the burger together with the tops of the buns and serve immediately.

SERVES: 4 FIREFIGHTERS

INGREDIENTS

1 lb. chicken thighs bone-in
1 cup of Soy Sauce
1/2 cup of brown sugar
2 tbsp. of Garlic
2 tsp. of ginger (fresh preferred or ground double)
1 tbsp. honey
4 green onions diced
1 tbsp. of sesame seeds for garnish

DIRECTIONS

Combine marinade with chicken let marinate for at least 30 minutes, but for optimal flavor, overnight in the refrigerator is best.

Grill chicken thighs for 2 minutes on each side and finish off in the oven at 350°F for 25 minutes or till internal temp of 165°F. Garnish with sesame seeds and diced green onions.

SERVES: 4 FIREFIGHTERS

CHICKEN TERIYAKI

RED WINE BRAISED SHORT RIBS

INGREDIENTS

5 pounds bone-in beef short ribs, cut crosswise into 2-inch pieces
Kosher salt and freshly ground black pepper
3 tbsp. vegetable oil
3 medium onions, chopped
3 medium carrots, peeled, chopped
2 celery stalks, chopped
3 tbsp. all-purpose flour
1 tbsp. tomato paste
1 750 ml bottle Cabernet Sauvignon
8 sprigs thyme
4 sprigs oregano
2 sprigs rosemary
1 head of garlic, halved crosswise
4 cups beef stock or chicken stock

DIRECTIONS

Preheat oven to 350°F. Season short ribs with salt, pepper, rosemary, oregano and thyme.
Heat oil in a large Dutch oven over medium-high. Working in batches, brown short ribs on all sides. Transfer short ribs to a plate. Add onions, carrots, and celery to the pot and cook over medium-high heat, stirring often, until onions are browned, about 5 minutes. Add tomato paste; cook, stirring constantly, until well combined and deep red, 2-3 minutes. Stir in wine, then add short ribs with any accumulated juices. Bring to a boil; lower heat to medium and simmer until wine is reduced by half, about 25 minutes. Stir in stock. Bring to a boil, cover, and transfer to oven. Cook until short ribs are tender, 2–2½ hours. Transfer short ribs to a platter. Strain sauce from pot into a measuring cup. Spoon fat from surface of sauce and discards; season sauce to taste with salt and pepper Place over garlic mash potatoes.

SERVES: 5 FIREFIGHTERS

BOMBERO SANDWICH (CUBAN)

- 1 - 8 inch Cuban Bread
- 5 oz ham lunch meat
- 8 oz pork shoulder steak
- ¼ cup of yellow mustard
- ¼ cup honey
- 1 tbsp. mayonnaise
- 1 tsp. red pepper
- ¼ cup diced dill pickles
- 3 slices of Swiss cheese
- 2 tsp. cup of butter
- 1 tsp. salt
- 1 tsp. pepper
- 1 tsp. adobo
- 1 tsp. garlic powder
- 1 cup of diced sweet onions
- 1 lime
- 1 lemon
- 1 orange
- 1 tbsp. cumin

1. Preheat the oven to 425° F.
2. In a small bowl, mix spices, garlic, salt, and pepper. Spread the mixture all over the pork shoulder.
3. Set the meat on a rack set into a roasting pan. Roast for 20 minutes, and then reduce the heat to 325° F. Continue to cook until an instant-read thermometer inserted into the shoulder reads 185° F, about 4 hours. Remove the pork from the oven and let stand until cool enough to handle, about 30 minutes.
4. Once out of the oven, cut into small squares, then take ham, pull apart and add to pork. In a skillet, add the pork and ham, and then add ¼ cup of mojo criollo. Sauté until meat is slightly browned. Take off heat to be used later.
5. Combine mustard/mayo/honey/red pepper then spread on Cuban bread
6. Then add dill pickles, followed by adding the meat in the skillet.
7. Add 3 slices of Swiss cheese and cover with the top of Cuban bread.
8. Place 1 tsp. of butter on flat pan allow to melt, then add Cuban sandwich and press with skillet till flatten. Flip over repeat until nice and flat.
9. Cut diagonally and Serve

SERVES: 3 FIREFIGHTERS

FIREHOUSE CHILI

INGREDIENTS

1 pound lean ground beef
1/2 pound chorizo sausage
1 onion, chopped
1 small green bell pepper, chopped
2 garlic cloves, minced
1 (8-ounce) can red kidney beans, rinsed and drained
1 (8-ounce) can black beans, rinsed and drained
3 tbsp. chili powder
1 tsp. salt
2 tsp. pepper
2 tsp. ground cumin
1 tbsp. of pureed chipotle pepper in adobo sauce or ground chipotle
1 (6oz. can) tomato paste
2 cup of beef stock
1 bundle of green onions. Chopped on diagonal.
1 cup of diced cooked bacon for garnish

DIRECTIONS

1. Dice the onion and bell pepper and mince the garlic.
2. Add to a large pot with the olive oil and cook over medium heat until they are soft and transparent.
3. Add the ground beef/chorizo continue to sauté until the meat is fully browned.
4. Add all the seasoning (chili, salt, pepper, cumin, chipotle)
5. Add tomato paste to the meat and stir.
6. Drain the beans and add them to the pot along with 2 cup beef stock.
7. Stir until well combined. Place a lid on the pot and allow it to simmer over a low flame for at least 15 minutes, stirring occasionally (the flavor gets better the longer it simmers). 8. Once finished, add the green onions, bacon, and cheese for garnish.

For alternatives
#Healthy: Replace meat with lean ground turkey and ground chicken breast/ Replace beef stock with chicken broth
#Vegetarian: Replace meat with shredded carrots/diced zucchini/squash/pinto Beans/ Replace stock with vegetable broth

SERVES: 6 FIREFIGHTERS

BLACKENED SALMON

INGREDIENTS

2 tbsp. ground paprika
1 tbsp. ground cayenne pepper
1 tbsp. onion powder
2 tsp. salt
1/2 tsp. ground white pepper
1/2 tsp. ground black pepper
1/4 tsp. dried thyme
1/4 tsp. dried basil
1/4 tsp. dried oregano
1/2 cup of butter
1lb. of salmon cut into 4 salmon fillets, skin and bones removed

DIRECTIONS

In a small mixing bowl, mix paprika, cayenne pepper, onion powder, salt, white pepper, black pepper, thyme, basil, and oregano.

Brush the 4 salmon fillets on both sides with 1/4 cup butter.

Rub evenly with the spice mixture on both sides of the fillet.
In a large, heavy skillet over medium high heat, cook salmon until blackened, 2 to 5 minutes. Turn fillets, drizzle with remaining butter, and continue cooking until blackened and fish is easily flaked with a fork.

SERVES: 4 FIREFIGHTERS

3rd Alarm Desserts & Breakfast

Congratulations! You've almost made it to the end, and I hope you're ready to sweeten things up. While we get ready to get some desserts going, let's talk about my third show: Food Network Star. Just like you at this point in the game, I'd gained confidence in my competitive chef skills by the time I earned a spot on Food Network Star. I was eager to share my personality with the world, and I knew exactly who I needed to beat for the win. I put together the best cooking show pilot I could and won third place. Can you believe it? Yep, me neither. I'll be honest, that one was a tough loss for me, and totally unexpected. But losses can't stop me, I was promoted to lieutenant that year and kept putting the flames on 'em. The competitive chef world has opened tons of doors for me to cook at firehouses all over the country, I cook for my local community every chance I get, and I've gained so many friends and fans all over the world. Believe me when I tell you, the love and support is truly unreal. That's life in the kitchen: you'll make mistakes every once in a while, but you'll come back with something even stronger (and more delicious), and the best friends are made over a good, sweet dish. Ready, set, let's make a few of the best desserts anyone has ever tasted. Say it with me:

Let's put some flames on 'em!

photo by Michael Moriatis

GUAVA BREAD PUDDING
w/ Marshmallow Sauce

INGREDIENTS

1/2 stick (4 tablespoons) butter
1 loaf brioche bread, cut into cubes
1 cup brown sugar
1 cup white sugar
1 tbsp. ground allspice
1 tbsp. ground cinnamon
1 tbsp. ground nutmeg
2 cups milk
5 large eggs
1/4 cup golden raisins
1/2 cup guava paste

Marshmallow-Vanilla Cream Sauce:
1 cup marshmallows
1/2 cup heavy cream
1/4 cup confectioners' sugar
1 tsp. vanilla extract

DIRECTIONS

For the guava bread pudding: Preheat the oven to 350° F. Grease a loaf pan with the butter.
In a large bowl, combine the brioche, 1/2 cup of brown sugar, white sugar,
allspice, cinnamon, nutmeg, milk, eggs, golden raisins, and guava paste. Mix well. Transfer to the prepared baking pan.
Bake until brown on top, about 45 minutes.
Cool on a rack.

For the marshmallow-vanilla cream sauce: Meanwhile, melt the marshmallows in a nonstick skillet over low heat. Add the heavy cream, confectioners' sugar and vanilla. Continue to cook over low heat, stirring, until the sauce comes together.
To serve, invert the bread pudding onto plate and spoon some sauce over the top

SERVES: 6-8 FIREFIGHTERS

MANNY'S CHEESECAKE

IINGREDIENTS

FOR THE CRUST
1-1/2 cups Biscoff cookies crumbs
4 tbsp. unsalted butter, melted
2 tbsp. sugar
Non-Stick Spray

FOR THE FILLING
32 oz. (four 8-oz blocks) cream cheese, at room temperature
2 cups sugar
3 tbsp. flour
4 tsp. vanilla extract
1 tsp. packed lemon zest, from 1 lemon
2 tsp. fresh lemon juice, from 1 lemon
5 large eggs
1/2 cup sour cream
Special equipment: 9-inch spring form pan

DIRECTIONS

Preheat oven to 325° F if using a silver 9-inch spring-form pan. Mix crumbs, 3 tbsp. sugar and butter; Add nonstick spray to springform pan ; press firmly into bottom of pan. Bake 10 minutes.
Beat cream cheese, sugar, flour, vanilla, lemon juice, and lemon zest with an electric mixer on medium speed until well blended. Add sour cream; mix well. Add eggs, 1 at a time, mixing on low speed after each addition just until blended. Pour over crust.
Bake 1 hour 10 minutes or until center is almost set. Run knife or metal spatula around rim of pan to loosen cake; cool before removing rim of pan.

* Use "Strawberry Sauce" from "Stuffed French Toast" as a topper
SERVES: 8 FIREFIGHTERS

POUND CAKE
w/ Fruit Flambé

INGREDIENTS

CAKE
3 sticks unsalted butter, softened
3 cups white sugar
2 tsp. vanilla extract, grated
1 tsp. almond extract
3/4 cup milk
5 eggs
3 cups all-purpose flour

FLAMBÉ
2 1/2 tbsp. butter
2 1/2 tbsp. brown sugar
¼ cup pineapple chunks, drained
1/2 cup dark rum
¼ cup of pitted cherries

DIRECTIONS

CAKE
Preheat oven to 350°F.
Using a stand mixer with the paddle attachment, cream butter and sugar together, on high, for 3 minutes. Add vanilla, almond, and milk to the mixture.
With the mixer speed on low, add flour and eggs alternating one at a time. Start and end with flour. Mix in eggs just until completely incorporated before adding flour each time. Be careful not to over-

Pour cake batter into a greased and floured bundt pan or loaf pan and bake for 60-70 minutes. Continue baking until a toothpick or cake tester is inserted and comes out clean.

FLAMBÉ
In a large skillet, cook the butter and brown sugar over medium heat, stirring, until the sugar dissolves. Place the pineapple in the syrup in a single layer, reduce the heat to medium-low, and cook for 3 to 4 minutes, until browned on the first side. Turn with a small spatula or tongs and cook on the second side until the pineapples are soft and richly browned. Add rum either with a match or flame from gas stove flambé.

SERVES: 8 FIREFIGHTERS

STUFFED FRENCH TOAST
w/ Strawberry Sauce

INGREDIENTS

CREAM CHEESE FILLING
8 ounces of cream cheese
1 cup powdered sugar
1 tsp. vanilla extract

FRENCH TOAST
12 slices brioche bread
7 large eggs
2 cups heavy cream
1 tsp. vanilla
1 cup of brown sugar
½ tbsp. cinnamon

STRAWBERRY SAUCE
1 lb. strawberries, rinsed, cut in half
1/3 cup granulated sugar
1 tbsp. lemon juice (from 1/2 Lemon)

DIRECTIONS

Beat the filling ingredient until smooth in a mixing bowl.
Spread a thick layer of filling on one side of half of the slices of bread. Top with remaining bread slices to form a sandwich.
Whisk the eggs, cream, cinnamon, brown sugar, and vanilla in a large mixing bowl;
set aside.
Spray some non-stick spray in a
casserole pan. Lay out the cream cheese stuffed

French Toast across the bottom of the casserole pan. Pour the egg mixture onto the French Toast. Let it sit for at least an hour preferably overnight if possible. Then simply bake it at 350°F for about 45 minutes or until the eggs are set.
In a medium saucepan, combine sliced strawberries, 1/3 cup sugar and 1 tbsp. fresh lemon juice. Place over medium heat and bring the mixture to a boil, stirring often. Reduce heat and simmer 15 minutes or until sauce is thickened, stirring occasionally.
Remove from heat and cool to room temperature.

SERVES: 6 FIREFIGHTERS

KEY LIME PANCAKES

INGREDIENTS

PANCAKE MIX
1 ½ cups all-purpose flour
3 ½ tsp. baking powder
1 tsp. salt
1 tbsp. white sugar
1 ½ cups buttermilk
1 egg
3 tbsp. butter, melted
2 tsp. vanilla extract
1 tsp. cinnamon

KEY LIME ICING
1/2 cup of confection sugar
2 tbsp. of sweetened condensed milk
2 tbsp. of lime juice

GARNISH
1/2 cup crushed Biscoff cookies
1 lime for lime zest

DIRECTIONS

To make the pancakes, simply mix together pancake mix.

Heat a nonstick skillet or pancake griddle and butter it. Pour the batter onto the hot griddle about ¼ cup at a time. When the top of each pancake bubbles, flip and continue cooking on the second side. Each cup of the mix will yield 4-6 pancakes.

Mix confection sugar, condensed milk, and lime juice to make the key lime icing. Add to pancakes then add cookies and lime zest to garnish.

SERVES: 4 FIREFIGHTERS

www.ingramcontent.com/pod-product-compliance
Lightning Source LLC
Chambersburg PA
CBHW042254100526
44589CB00002B/19